DICHTEN =
No. FIVE

D1714926

OSKAR PASTIOR

MANY
GLOVE COMPARTMENTS

SELECTED POEMS

translated from the German by
Harry Mathews
Christopher Middleton
Rosmarie Waldrop

with a guest appearance by John Yau

 BURNING DECK, PROVIDENCE, 2001

DICHTEN = is a (not quite) annual of current German writing in English translation. Most issues are given to the work of a single author. Editor: Rosmarie Waldrop.

Individual copies: $10
Subscription for 2 issues: $16
In England: £5.
Subscription for 2 issues: £8. Postage 25p/copy.

Distributors:
Small Press Distribution, 1341 Seventh St., Berkeley, CA 94710
1-800/869-7553; orders@spdbooks.org
Spectacular Diseases, c/o Paul Green, 83b London Rd., Peterborough, Cambs. PE2 9BS

for US subscriptions only:
Burning Deck, 71 Elmgrove Ave., Providence RI 02906

Some of the translations were first printed in the following magazines. Harry Mathews: *Exact Change Yearbook, Schreibheft, The Paris Review, TO*; Christopher Middleton: *Agenda, Chicago Review, Dimension, Shearsman*, and in his collection, *Faint Harps & Silver Voices* (Carcanet, 2000); Rosmarie Waldrop: *American Letters & Commentary, Aufgabe, Bombay Gin, Chicago Review, Denver Quarterly, Kenning, Untitled*.

This volume is published with the help of a translation subsidy by Inter Nationes, Bonn.
Burning Deck is the literature program of Anyart: Contemporary Arts Center, a tax-exempt (501c3), non-profit corporation.

Cover by Keith Waldrop

ISSN 1077-4203
ISBN 1-886224-44-7

CONTENTS

INTRODUCTORY NOTE

"It is as if we heard Adam and Eve breathing, as if the leaves were rustling on the tree of knowledge, as if the serpent hissed, in short, as if first and last things were engaged in conversation." So Dieter Roth describes Oskar Pastior's work. Paradisal perhaps, but not adamic. Unlike Adam (whom he calls "the old Stalin of language")* Pastior is not out to name animals or anything else. "Talking *about* things is not possible. Language, the text, speaks itself —this is the great dilemma to which theories of realism (always indifferent to language and languages) close their eyes."

For Pastior, language itself is the stuff of life, a metabolism where words and even concepts are made flesh. He explores it through puns, lists, strings, heaps, fields, dictionaries, alphabets, collage, montage, potpourris — all in orgiastic expansion. The result is "thought-music as a leaping perspective" — a perspective, in which a successful "nonsensical" text like "ur-cur trusts sulfur baths: plush" (p. 90) "is infinitely more precise than this kind of statement."

Again, what interests him in palindromes is the ontological moment where we realize "whether, when, and that (hence how) the text builds itself up into a palindrome and, both divided and gathered by the reading, runs in two directions even though it appears one-dimensional; whether, when and that (hence how) it signifies what constitutes it — among other things a palindrome — and constitutes what signifies it."

Translation? Not possible, says Pastior. It is "the wrong word for a process that does not exist. In a different language you think differently, speak differently, act differently, are different." So, like the "whole problem of reading and writing and interpretation...it comes down to the measly connective *and*: A text *and* a text."

Only a fraction of Pastior's poems allow even such a second text to be set beside his. This selection lays no claim to being representative. There are whole genres which none of us translators attempted, e.g. Pastior's anagram poems or the letter-based palindromes, like our "Madam I'm Adam," but only some that work with the larger units of word or line (pp. 93-96). There are only a few samples of the highly formalist work: e.g. poems that use only one vowel (pp. 89, 90) and "vocalises," where each line has the same sequence of vowels (pp. 92, 104). Here the first question is whether to base the English version on the letter or on its pronunciation. Then comes the challenge to use as much of the semantic dimension of the original words as possible — while making the pattern work in English.

Likewise in "dominotaurus" (p. 102), a game of dominos where words that overlap in one syllable (domino, minotaurus, usbekistan, androgyne, gynecologist...) coalesce into one monstrous compound.

Mostly, we hope that our versions, if they cannot keep the impossible promise of translation, will at least approximate the pleasure of Pastior's texts.

Rosmarie Waldrop

---

*Quotations are from *Das Unding an sich: Frankfurter Vorlesungen* (Suhrkamp, 1994) and an interview in Edith Konradt, *Oskar Pastior* (Verlag Wissenschaft & Politik, 1993).

I. HEARBAGE:

Sixty Broadcasts from One
Frequency Band

Höricht:
Sechzig Über-
tragungen aus einem
Frequenzbereich
(Klaus Ramm) 1975——

PLEASE KEEP YOUR proper from this announcement; multiply this distance, selectively, by the following prizes: first three unlived lives, second two unlived lives, third one unlived life. With the result raise the article of faith most proper to yourself to the status of a triangle and you obtain the dignity that befits you. If during the first three weeks after receipt you send this to us on a postcard, you will be joining in the live broadcast in the series TO EACH HIS OWN, and you will obtain a lot entitling you to waive the draw. Do not forget the prize you selected. It tips you off.

C. M.

HIFI-HEARBAGE IS SPUN exceedingly fine. The listener hears the sound produced by his ear hearing sounds made by his radio emitting sounds made by the station sending HiFi-hearbage sending sounds made by the tape played for this purpose playing sounds made by the microphone recording sounds made by the ear of the recorded person hearing sounds made by a great calm swallowing smaller calms.

R. W.

FIRST SENTENCE: The rage over the lost dime manifests itself on a level of sense that knows no rage. Second sentence: We all know the example of the summer guest put through the meatgrinder, who at first pretended to be deaf in order not to spoil the sport, but our gooseflesh knows no such limit. Third sentence: Add the report on the Bethlehem innocents slain and quartered on the grounds that a single flight presents too high a risk, a credible insurance policy, especially as the painting reassembles afterward. Fourth sentence: Rounded off is the impression of the street fight of that century, to which our outlaw village owes its gently melancholic name of Rombola; hammer, anvil, stirrup. Coda: Well, now various semaphores overlap on a level that gives no quarter. Mourning over lost gooseflesh knows no limit. A single exhibition presents too high a risk, better to spread it among generations of Rombolas. A credible meatgrinder, especially as the century reassembles afterward.

R. W.

SO, "AN INVENTION concerning speech." No, I object, rather behave as if the invention were an exercise acquired at a bad moment and better kept in a safe. Far from being a case of casuistry, loose talk of an invention concerning speech is the kind of activity we shall designate by blue. After all, aerial shocks such as these we always furnish with a high-explosive apartment kitchen, "but transition in breathing is not our business." Oh, Oh, you logical subjects. It seems indeed convincing that an invention should be as convinced of itself as if it were an exercise concerning swimming acquired at a bad moment, which we shall designate by blue. Or the strange behavior concerning the existence of an ice-egg inside a roasting Alaska rooster, which we shall designate by that very invention concerning speech.

R. W.

"THE WRONG TROUT" is quadrophonic hearbage addressed exclusively to listeners with quadruple ears. At the beginning the wrong trout sings a right song. Then a right wanderer sings a wrong song. Protest against the wrong trout's right song is registered from the wrong side. Followed by praise for the right wanderer's wrong song from the right side. Whereupon trout and wanderer trade songs, but sing them from the wrong end. The following wrongheaded protest against the wrong-endedness of the songs comes, it is true, from the right side, but confuses the songs, whereas the immediately following praise of the wrongheaded protest comes from the right side, but rubs wrong. Hereafter trout and wanderer sing together "Free as a bird in the air," but with interchanged parts so that the following protest cannot be told apart from the simultaneously following praise. Then a wrong wanderer and a right trout are introduced with a song each, and quadrophonics triumphs on all sides.

R. W.

IN MY MEMORY of a certain hearbage disturbance there occurs the name of an unimportant city. It turns out to be the city that has established a contemporary office for the investigation of certain disturbances in the field of memory. The city is unimportant because such offices exist also in other cities. It is true that those do not bear the name of this city, and it is precisely this name that disturbingly occurs in my memory of a certain hearbage disturbance. On the other hand, the office in this city is contemporary, i.e. it comes and goes like certain memories in the field of the disturbances it investigates. The connection with hearbage exists independently from and yet only through this office, just as the certain hearbage disturbance certainly triggers the memory in which occurs the name of the unimportant city, but at the same time causes in it, in memory, this disturbance which, being contemporary, comes within the field of memory of the office in this city whose name is unimportant. Hence hearbage in itself must be considered an important un-contemporary process even though only its disturbance triggers anything worth mentioning.

R. W.

TWICE UPON A TIME it was tomorrow. Twice upon a time it was different from what it would have been tomorrow. Twice the birds did not scream, once without effort, the other time regardless of damage. It is so difficult, at three in the morning, to listen to birds screaming without effort and regardless of damage. Nor did we twice fare differently, tomorrow and tomorrow, twice each.

R. W.

THE CATCHASCATCHER cardinals again through groves and woods. He forges ahead, so the story goes, a taste of venison on his tongue, girded with sensuality, a twitter in his ear, elasticity in the tendon area, eye unsheathed and oleofactual, in short, in short. If you once meet him you never catch up. Nobody has met him a second time. Only in the snapshots managed now and then surreptitiously through a cane or brim-flap by mushroom-picking journalists, does the catchascatcher open one drafty mouth while his other is champing, glittering, melodic, polaroid. From far-off chasms, an echo: cahee, cahee.

R. W.

THE SKYBLUE BUDGERIGARLIC sits on a garlic mountain and simulates a skyblue budgerigarlic. In fact, he is a renovation project for certain areas of cultivation. Shyly the gleaners in the Millet valley raise their clear watery eyes to the rim of their bonnets and hiss: "Cozy ness! Ah see mouse! Tangent y'all! O Canaletto!" This relieves him of his primal matter but not of the ephemeral. He itches, he scratches, he acts most rootish, yea heretically. He gives evidence that follows from other pieces of evidence and would be proved along with their proof if he did not just sit here like this, the rascal on the lam.

R. W.

19

YOU ARE LISTENING to hearbage by Jacob and Sillis. You are listening to what you do not wish to listen to, but listen because I say you are listening. You do not wish to listen to hearbage by Jakob and Sillis because I say you do not wish to listen to it. But if I say you are listening to what you do not wish to listen to, namely hearbage by Jakob and Sillis, I don't say this at random, but to you. I say to you, you do not wish to listen to what you are listening to because you wish to listen to what you are not listening to, i.e. not this hearbage, because it is not your wish to listen to something you cannot listen to because you only wish to listen to it that says, but rather it is I that say to you, you wish to listen to what you are not listening to because you do not wish to listen to what you are listening to. I say to myself, you say to yourself you do not wish to listen to hearbage by Jakob and Sillis. You say to yourself, I say to myself I want to persuade you to listen to it anyway. I say to myself, you say to yourself,I say to myself you do not wish to listen to this hearbage because you say to yourself, I say to myself you do not wish to listen to it so that I can convince you that you have already been listening to it for some time. However, this is probably wrong. You have been listening to hearbage by Jakob and Sillis.

R. W.

IF IN RESHINAR the street sweepers have either two right or two left legs, then Reschinar is very remote from other mountain villages. In the course of generations, the swing of the brooms has bent the standing leg into a moving one and the moving leg into a standing one or, rather, has shortened and stretched both into a double-legato, a posture reminiscent of the Folies-Bergères, but which must rather be called a leftover of feudal-antifeudalism. The retrograde theory of sunk culture does not sit well with them, on the contrary, the quiet syncretism manifest in the dance-like execution of their professional obligation marks the intersection of latent trends from the Carpatho-Pannonic toward the Catalan sphere of influence, both vaulted, and vice versa. Only the Dracula version, which they themselves call stuff and nonsense, transplants their working tool to the salons. An objectively musical process that truly touches the heart.

R. W.

WHEN A RARE BEAST jumps through a rare object it causes suction in which the rareness of the beast and the rareness of the object fuse into rare beauty. The result is called beautiful impulse. It fuses with suction, which makes other rare beasts jump through rare objects. Repetition is the mother of contradiction. She owns a circus and waves impulses about. Through the cupola there whistles suction caused by common beasts jumping through common objects. The result is called beautiful resistance.

R. W.

THE DRIPPING FAUCET is, from beginning to end, hearbage of speech exclusively. First, a trembly voice announces the theme. It consists of a monosyllabic drip-word modeled on the drip of a dripping faucet resp. the word-drop that is its evident annulment. Whereupon single voices, some ringing like bells, some breaking, in turn repeat the theme consisting of the drip-word resp. word-drop, reinforcing its memorable character. Whereupon a sonorous voice improvises a version of the task to be accomplished by convincingly scanning the theme. Other voices join in and offer other takes. An emotional voice interjects shrill, sobering accents. This hearbage goes on and on. Again and again the vocal artists put their most stringent efforts into thematically tolerated, yea enthusiastically fostered monosyllables. They sing and swing, they con- and polyverse, they concentrically move onto the blind spot of the method to be applied, the as it were shaved-off linden leaf on the microphone's kidney. The task amplifies audibly while the monosyllabic drip-word modeled on the drip of a dripping faucet respectively the word-drop that is its obvious annulment does not stop being heard in this hearbage.

R. W.

NEWS OF THE WILDFIRE spreads rapidly toward the weekend. In a moment it'll have the sleeper in the graph at blade-point. Already it arouses the vital spirits. Ah, how ripe the nose, how merrily fever makes hay in the graph of Dürer's *Kleines Rasenstück.* I too have something to say on this topic. Boy, how we used to lie in the graph, the trench graph, with the reservoir, the gas stations, the fuel pumps! Why don't you say something? Who wants to say nothing on this topic? Wheeling-dealing, for instance, sharpens the sense of geographic distances. My epicenter is more ready for a vacation than hers; it sits in the hollow of my knee and tickles every five seconds. His, on the other hand, smolders along pompously. I know families whose blood jumps with sugar. A crisis every five seconds, why don't you say something. What, no outbreak of family liability in no congested area? No mitten muddle? No burning of hostages, no sum total whatever in seatbelts? I'd really be surprised, with all this demand on the weekends. Every five graphhoppers the fire alarm goes off. Please do say something.

R. W.

THE HEARBAGE THAT has been traced back all the way to Arhitchcophanes consists of a closed room filled with free-rising, free-floating and free-falling dactyls. Dactyls are recurrent hand-and-mouth signs of one stressed and two unstressed syllables each, of which the last is always more distressed than the preceding or following. This regularly irregular fluttering makes them momentarily tangible. They have the form of eccenterprises, cowcatcherrails, and smashed flytime-pieces. Others remind us of three-partite memories. Others again cannot be touched, but emit a pulsating odor. The dactyls are connected to the closed room in which they exist, but nevertheless aspire to their end. The more they twitch, the more strangely they rise, float, fall, the harder to tell apart. In vain do the war-doves try, by cooing caesuras and pauses, to escape this state of hearbage which is based on a Viennese Waltz and named after them.

R. W.

WHEN YOU SAY THAT a voice translates the breath of catastrophe-spin, you really mean to say catastrophe wastes its breath on a voice that is less voice than information about airplanes and so on. But when you say this, you actually translate a vocal exercise into slowly interrupted breath-basis from which evolve bodies on wheels, and rose stains spread in sentences till the onset of porfirogenesis, that is to say, a silence wasted on catastrophe. And where, you ask, breathes the rejoinder, the verdigris behind the gesture? Or take the academic runway, the butchery of concussed air, the sudden interpolation of reality on wheels! Always, so a voice translates the breath of spin, backwards the spin of breath translates a voice.

R. W.

HEARING MUSIC sets time free in the ear: the ear produces free time. This insight is the basis of lease-an-ear, a thriving service branch. The free time generated with the help of leased ears can be stored, for instance on tape, which constantly augments the sum of free time because nothing is ever lost. Last year alone, on a world scale, free time reserves of the magnitude of 350 000 music-years were stored — just imagine! The most difficult problems of free time occur when leased free time does not find an ear because the ear that could produce it has already been leased out and is setting free time free elsewhere. Lease your ear to music!

R. W.

THEN PASQUALE GALUPPI heard neither the following nor anything else of which it could be said in sounds that he, Pasquale Galuppi, had ever heard it. To make clear what happened and is still happening, Pasquale Galuppi would have to tell us in sounds: I, Pasquale Galuppi, heard and am still hearing a story in sound, that is to say: I am so molested by the sound of this story that this is what I think. But Pasquale Galuppi does not tell us this nohow. Who are we, anyway? And what happened and is still happening is, after all, I must say, molestation, nothing but molestation.

R. W.

———————— INTERLUDE

AUTOBIOGRAPHICAL TEXT

Although my father was not only a teacher of drawing but also died later, my mother, in Transylvania as well as in the year that should prove crucial for my future life, nevertheless gave birth to me.

Similarly complex states of affairs have increasingly become the reason that I not only write poems but also no others.

Perhaps this is all connected to the fact that in school — Plato's school of course, where you speak whenever and it blossoms — I didn't pay enough attention to the relation of crime and punishment to war and peace (like novels, on the one hand, but, on the other, biographi- and reciprocal respectively), especially because I worked the graveyard shift among the boilers in order to acquire a bit of history and immunity against cause and effect.

Later I was a crate nailer, cement mixer, construction estimate calculator in a curly wooded and undulating landscape associated with music. In short, what I can say about myself will later (when scrutinized for meaning) turn out to be artificial, i.e. composed. Of course I later went to the university in Bucharest and even worked for the radio. As a reporter, however, I was weak.

Nevertheless, even after some larger geographic skips and insights, I still feel funny, i.e. get freelance goose- and hobo-flesh when I say "I'm a poet" — let alone "Ergo sum." Suspect, suspect. For of all the cognitive business that I keep books on, some is lacking, to be sure, but even the forms to be filled out are sloppy and far from complete.

Otherwise I herewith declare that I am less good at nailing butter crates than at nailing eggplant crates — I once got up to 800 nails an hour. Long live the eggplant crate, it is one of the beauties of nature.

"Differentiation is good."

Yes, I dig down into memory. Chips. Slivers. Anecdotes. When, for instance, the offspring listens to parental conversation and catches the phrase: "...they'll skin me," and soberly pictures the scene: his progenitor nailed upside down to the door, his skin, a rabbitskin in shreds, pulled down over his ears. What do you mean misunderstood? Can sentences be wrong? No, in the biographical context, my bloody horror picture still has the cognitive value of a poem, and it doesn't matter if I like it or not — I still talk with this sentence, even now, from head to toe, they'll have to skin me, again and again, lilac, shellac LP, nothing else. What I remember is old hats, hits, headlines, mascots whose aura pervades the words I use.

To track down differences through description, whereby the instrument of investigation, language, is cruder and at the same time finer than the object which it not only investigates but also brings about and presents: the description, thus and only thus differentiation. Yet: there is no total description. And every investigation falsifies the result. This impossibility remains as sting, perhaps as motor.

(*Ingwer und Jedoch*, Herodot, 1985)

R. W.

II. POEMS 1960-80

IRISH RIVER FROM THE 8TH CENTURY

A Kingdom for a Horse, a Horse, a Horse,
A Soul for a deeply Sleep. And
Wallenstein's astrologer in the second house of the sun
what is the meaning of favored in love?
And in the lab watch out for five-footed iambs.
Sara begat Jevo. Jevo begat Mira
and Mar, Cain and Abel, Dach and Au and Schwitz.
Au in turn begat Naga and Hiro and Kyb.
And visited obedience on their children
unto the fourth generation. There arose a
there flowed down a there opened up
an Irish river from the eighth century,
A Kingdom for a Soul, for a Horse, for a Sleep.

R. W.

WHO COMES HERE SO MORNING-FRESH?
Who mornings here so freshly come?
Who freshes here so morningly?
Comes here who fresh the morning so?
Who comes here morn who nings here fresh?
Who nings so morn who heres so come?
Who heres who meres who so?
Comes here so who?
Morns who so where?
Who here?
Mourn

R. W.

FROM ONE STING TO AN-
other and the oriole fell into
the frying pan from the fire
that was still in Pilate's time
since then untwittered's been the wide
from one blue to another sky
from man to Mantua and
many a cradle to the gravy
from farenwide to longenback
to a night's rest from catharso
came the prof to the proof
and the mountain to the profiterole
from the long and snort of it
to light to a head to bacco to day
came the oriole to nothing

R. W.

POEMPOEMS ARE SLIGHTLY more different from paper than paper is from them in this margin lie the opportunities and miseries of the one as well as of the others POEMPOEMS can only be compared to things that bear comparison and to that degree they are obligatory as inventions they are subject to obsolescence as german text however they act unlike theory for example they serve many purposes and have the last laugh on their backside whenever there is silence the muses do battle

R. W.

IN THE POEM THERE ARE: 1 morning 1 woman 1 gunesch 1 how 1 are you 1 middle 1 spuds on the other hand in the poem there are not: 1 pardon 1 mr. 1 schoger 1 we 1 know 1 that's how 1 people 1 are both the words that are in the poem and the words that are not in the poem have an endoctrinal frequency index of $1 = 0$ whence the relevant relation between the words that are in the poem and the words that are not in the poem whose unutterability has entered secondary literature as the unutterable put simply let us consider what the poem would be without the words that are not in the poem the poem would be a popular one

R. W.

WHEREAS IN THE FIRST LINE the puppy assists his master in drowning in the second line there is no longer any hope of rescue the third line grows desperate whereas help is already on the way in the fourth line the poem demonstrates FIDELITY whereas its title ALREADY points toward the universal

R. W.

THE SHIVERPOEM SHIVERS at the thought it might consist in a speech process claiming to contain a thought process that had become so independent that its speech process would shiver at the very thought of shivering the shiverpoem is silly to think so because how can one shiver at the mere thought of shivering

R. W.

IN THE FIRST LINE there is an A and another A they are the two A's of the first line in the second line there is an A and another A they are the two A's of the first line but in reverse order in the third line there is an A and another A they are no longer the two A's of the first line but the two A's of the fourth line although in reverse order this becomes clear in the fourth line where there is an A and another A i.e. the two A's of the fourth line although not in reverse order the poem can be read horizontally and vertically which makes for a stupendous increase of effect please copy

R. W.

THE CALECHE OF POETRY is expected to arrive in the eponymous allegorical poem its opponent is the shell of the world also represented are the history of symbols the symbol of thought the thought of freedom and the freedom of the shell a genitive errant undresses among the rules for error positioned in the background is the caleche with persons positioned inside it is approaching

BRIDAL COACH

bridal coach stops
bridegroom heads into the bushes
bride dreams of brief rain
forest makes a scene

from the bushes a dog's head
from the bushes a calf
a calf with a dog's head
nobody's watching

forest sad
forest makes poem:

"Calf with dog's head is evil
Prikulitsch
all afraid
all look on"

from the bushes
nobody sees the rain
nobody sees brief rain
nobody bridal caleche
exit nobody in coach
bird from the left:

"Prikulitsch Prikulitsch!"

he who reads this
has read it

R. W.

CARNAL PLEASURE (SENIOR) and Carnal Pleasure (junior) are rowing across a lake in a boat. The boat is made of white cottonwool. They are on a firm excursion, because Carnal Pleasure and Carnal Pleasure are in business together. They are rowing for publicity, because Carnal Pleasure and Carnal Pleasure manufacture cottonwool, for various ends. Carnal Pleasure and Carnal Pleasure in a cottonwool boat, it might be a game of clouds played in a mirror, a card game peculiar to the Lake of the Four Forests, up and down. Who'll sting? Carnal Pleasure and Carnal Pleasure are bathed in a rosy hue; that is due to rowing and to the effulgence of the bights they are rowing in. Even the distant glaciers proclaim the firm's flesh; even the industrious cows, now glazed with lilac, made of deseeded cottonwool, graze on their behoof. Father and son row with Tampax and Q-Tips. They are highly satisfied, it was a great publicity campaign. In the water a light rises up; then something in the sky goes strange.

C. M.

THE EFFECT GROUNDLESSNESS HAS when points of concentration are traversed does not suddenly show but unexpectedly recedes. Reporter hastily present: "When did the thought come to you?" No reply — also a reply? Actually it's not sure that thoughts come while you go walking away; they do the walking, burps through footsoles, an abstruse notion of the legs, one after the other, in the walking we do. A recession, across hollows, shafts, drains, a downflow into the cable-naveling. One might say: a kind of earthing comes, but, as already said, it just goes, leaking through toenails. A sort of receding, that is what a thought is.

C. M.

THE GOURMET IS A TORMENTED MAN. He sees himself regularly transported into indescribable rooms. Somehow it turns out that there is a hatch somewhere, leading into a kitchen. In passing he hears about the presence of the table at which, how shall one say it, for days he has been sitting. He does not let this confuse him; he's a gourmet. A girl serves flowers of some kind in a sophisticated coiffure. A fellow-diner is leaning against the mantlepiece. "Just look at the trees," something advises him, something later addressed by something else as "johann." While he is taking the advice, the dining room, for that is what it is, like the pneumatic elevator in Lomonossow University suddenly whizzes up like lightning to the tenth floor. The street is an abysm of giddiness. At precisely this moment the tiny red cap of a pie-deliverer passes through the main entrance. The sea, of which it was said between some second and third course or other that it "nestled" against the city from the south, must thus be to (plus dative) his "mind" actually in the east, because the pie-deliverer came into the house, now with its ten floors and overlooking the harbor, by the main entrance; unless, of course, the conservatory, of which some fellow-diner or other said that one could smell in it, in spite of the humid rubber-plants, the "ozone of pagan dread" (which, as the gourmet, or else he'd not be one, is for some reason one hundred percent certain creeps westward down the valleys from the northern plateaus), really were located in that sector of the house which is reached through the reception room. That could actually be the case, if the seventh course were served from the rightrightleft. But that is where the wall is, and the seventh course is not served up; it is steaming, but where? The gourmet is a tormented man, the seating-plan is altogether illusory, someone is clearing his throat, his direction-finding nose wanders around, the hatch is now inside his head, the table (cleared) is at eye-level, covering itself with the horizon of the blue sea, also with the pursed lips of the lady portrayed in oils. It strikes the gourmet consequently that the pie-deliverer's office must be "right next door." Through open nostrils pointing toward midnight pours unsated ozone.

C. M.

44

CHEESE STRUDEL, WHISPERS Griselda, is the continuation of instruction with other means. And the variation of a dictum, counters Vanilla, is like a novel by Tolstoy: you think you're reading, but you devour. Let alone life! Raisin puts in her two cents' worth. Life is the continuation of cheese strudel with war and peace, it all depends on the proportionality of means. Twilight zone, says Laokoon, eyewash with pasta, but, as Griselda said, a kind of instruction. The cheese strudel was gone. Thereupon the four made love, with other means, true, but the smell was delicious.

R. W.

45

BALLAD OF THE DEFECTIVE CABLE

Adafactave
Caybl
It rmbls cataractish-lish
Uatafawls
aalsobrawns Brambl
aalso dooes

Slautter im
slautter im
zeohn son

In Uatafawls

Haswegottem?
Gottem
Aintgottem
noway

Its jst a dafactave
rmbln
traktats
a neddershtilzt
Rompl-Grompt

Caybl O Caybl watta
Caybl wesgot!

Gifus an
adakuat Ch-pell
sosto klearr
ze trumpln Bvchuelltr
outa our
naavl

R. W.

FRESCOBALDI

I am an opposite of am. Am is an op-
posite of is. An opposite is a teahouse
by me. Together with an opposite I

am raw brick of am or a teahouse of is.
This isn't all that complicated. Is is a
teahouse in Celle. Without a teahouse

Celle is raw brick. An opposite of Cel-
le is an adagio, that is with me in raw
brick. But also with Bruno! Together

with Bruno Celle is a system of am.
Together with me Bruno is raw brick
by Scharoun. With and without Celle

an adagio with Bruno is a teahouse by
me without teahouse — an opposite
is a system without is, only am. But I

am not as complicated as together with
Bruno in raw brick. Without Celle a tea-
house in Celle is without is — it is an

adagio of am or raw brick without oppo-
site in an opposite without system or Bru-
no without Bruno in a teahouse by me.

R. W.

47

O MAGDALEN!

The town in which my capacity for thought is
frittered away is a large, proud, round town.
The thought of horse is not, e.g., part of it.

This town which is my one and all consisting of
two halves of Merseburg is called also Merseburg,
because, even if I do think of horse, something

not part of it, maybe, my one and all is dimin-
ished in it; and consists of two large, proud
hemispheres, because these hemispheres fall

apart if my horses run out of breath. Right
there at the gates of my town, which gates are
held together by spells, there the horses sweat

and strain. They use up a lot of breath. When
Merseburg falls apart at both Merseburg gates,
it is either daytime or it is night. I

need day as well as night time for thinking —
which makes me run out of breath. My town in
which breath runs out combines not only phy-

sics, but also the horses, to think of which is
not part of it — they heave and split, it's
then I think that my capacity for thought runs

out. When the proud hemispheres fall apart, I
think, even the proud words run out of force
and one and all departs — to the northnorthsouth.

C. M.

OF SCIENCE AND RESEARCH

Symmetry, with me, consists in an axis
which, erect, runs sometimes here and
sometimes there. Then everything grows

double from my side: the leg, the skin, the
tearduct, right hand, chin, varieties of
hair. Promptly a second eye bulges from

the head — which, like a lettuce leaf, grows
first two, then twice two, then twice twice two
and yet more icicles. Sufficient unto naked

existence are sixty-four fields. True, one hip
by now sits in mid-belly — the other belly is,
in compensation, held as a knife to

the throat. Then Wednesday in profile: through
holes that, it is true, are no such thing and vanish
fast — they're flight cocks, air corridors in-

verted — I owe it to the world that much in it
occurs at the same time. And, when the mail
arrives, the moment of rotation. Holidays

spread hypotheses: one rag here, one rag on
top, sandwich style — two antedated green
branches on head. It's true we need to add

an appendix, disheveling of the earth's shadow,
da Vinci's scrotumnal tilt, Minerva's rainbow-
udder — symmetry so often is sublime.

R. W.

ON MY SLEEP

It used to be that, when I went to sleep, sleep came.
Now, when sleep comes I'm already fast asleep.
Sleep used to come later, now I'm asleep sooner.

When I'm fast asleep it may happen that sleep,
when it comes, wakes me up once more before
I go on being fast asleep. It used to be this way:

I slept, and sleep came. Only when I woke up
it was gone again — unquiet guest. Now it
comes and goes a bit more quietly while I

sleep, and sometimes it is suddenly there when
I'm awake. Then I wake up and see it's there. Then
sleep keeps running through my mind, as now,

I cannot go to sleep before it goes: then it has
got to come. In this way it is now quite unlike
the way it used to be. It comes and it goes, I

wake I sleep. There's much runs through my mind
which, unlike the way it used to be, is less and less
like sleep: it too comes and goes, it too wakes me

now and then, while in my thoughts I watch it
sleep before sleep comes, this unquiet quiet
that knows no sleep, not even when I wake.

R. W.

INTERLUDE

TEXT

Text has less text than together with a reader. Text has also more texts than readers. Text however has also more text than texts and less readers than without a reader — such imprecision, and always at the wrong moment. Because if text more or less has or is it nevertheless is much that it has nothing to do with. It cannot choose the wrong moment even though it is more text than reader and has more text than texts. Between it and its texts and between it and its reader there happens more text than at the wrong moment — this at least is less an incident with debacle than an accident without proper text. Point by point, the text is sealed, soldered shut by its texts. Point by point no text becomes text. In the reader's head it is not where the reader's head is for the moment in question. In which incredibly much happens, i. e. not this way, precisely.

Has and is because what is projected onto it does not jive, because it jives differently in the projection and the non-projection because, if the projection that does not jive becomes another projection, it suddenly — horrors! — has a poetics which is less its own than that of one of its texts or of one of its readers without it.

Has and is, therefore, when its making does not catch up with it — The Beautiful Lemma, The Beautiful Slf, The Beautiful Scrap. Who and what meets where and whom: Lambda to Kuweit and Luna according to position — here Archibald, here O the glyph! The material in the bottled moment — the fish in the slate.

All sorts of raw text: the lopsided hole as ur-cheese or chees-ura before and after the cheese but rather more after (iamiam). These symptomatics of silly symptoms as a warning against welcoming the text — hey! Confronted with the logic of arrant understanding even the craftiest warning functions grow pale, likewise the cunning of its menetekel hobbyhorse "not about — but itself." Stocked, documented, evokes its expulsion through incorporation (be yond the pale! inglobulation) — alas that phages and paths are so rare. Implicit in howlers and jowlers recently a more serious category. Disarming let him be please to the point of impudence, in short politically educational, spread open, in short erotic, a different matter, in short relevant, getting under the skin, hence dermatologically challenged, and for all that no more than a private letter, you know, a miserable scrawl etc.

Text has less text than together with a reader. Its secret. Text need not be good or text. Its lack of necessity. Of course it needs other texts. That's its morality. Also, it never misses no stupid words. That is its misunderstanding.

(Jalousien aufgemacht, Carl Hanser, 1987)

R. W.

52

III. READINGS WITH TINNITUS

Lesungen mit
Tinnitus
(Carl Hanser) 1986 ——

—brief ode for ef fon o 55
—olican and pelican... 56
—with brass and band... 57
—beery cycling hoary train... 58
—a desert with high heels 59
—it's on dry cohesion... 60
—he who is without least acid... 61
—crimean-gothic marching song 62
—shocks in the mason jar 63
—idem 64
—what, however... 65
—the construction is simple... 66
—the fusion began... 67
—many glove compartments 68
—training for smaller buildings 69
—ammonite anonymous 70
—candide 71
—one molecule tinnitus... 72
—within the meaning of... 73
—there's a smell... 74
—mole in profil 75
—mausoleum... 76
—filling station 77
—apping 78
—in front of... 79
—raven son 80
—a plot 81

BRIEF ODE FOR EF FON O

o fadda mine son — on saddaday
grandmodda oh — mine bandaid yoo
won day i to america. america, oh?
i say goodday — o sunshine mine!

mine o mine stubbornness dat she before
where dragonflies flie — in garden-
house. yoo just — mine breast and den
on radio wafes — whiteout and bladderwort...

for yoo i haf brooms dree — anakreon
yer chilthood pix oh hony chilt
won day by seat of mine italian pants
read ofid too— oh how so ofish oh

R. W.

OLICAN AND PELICAN present an offering — under the oxygen tent. Olican to Pelican: "Alcibiades!" Pelican to Olican: "Plasma-lynx!" What magnificent chest-busters. We watch the transfusion business. What magnificent loudspeakers. We hear: "Mistral!" feeds "Fetus!" "Fetus!" throws himself at the feet of "O you agglutinative summertime!" "Onomastic bolt!" eats his heart out. These are not our feelings, they are only called that. "Take your places — bite — down!"... "Your forehead — my chest!"... (Alcibiades to Pelican, Plasma-lynx to Olican, Fetus coddles Mistral, Castor blows Pollux, Eboli and Stromboli cluck.) Under the celestial tent a smell of black gummibears, oxygen ramified.

R. W.

WITH BRASS AND BAND, tinnitus on the Rhine. It's no carnival, it's no overall, it's nothing but a dragon-green earwig — and merry free-for-all!... we hear so much about the Rhine. My father who a foxtail was, my mother who a woolfish was, all Greek to me a mouse king was — and it's all tinnitus to me... By hearsay tinnitus is an asparagus-hyacinth. Its hammer that an anvil was, its anvil that a jammer was, its stir up — Pig Latin. Its grammar has behindhand bracketed its iamb... Bubbles are rising, tandaradei. Tinnitus brassy and randy: cut class! cut class!

R. W.

BEERY CYCLING, HOARY TRAIN, airy flex! Hairy
moulade, leary dundancy, dairy busses — nary an
armament of mince, marmalade blocks story sistance
in the square... On all fours gory mates dinary animals
from Addis Abeba to Fürth. The barker the birch the
stunger the bung — headwind, steady tory proaches.
For ordinarks are neither handy tectives nor show
ordinary spect: antiphlox, ilophone...

R. W.

A DESERT WITH HIGH HEELS

entities and looking beyond them — lenses
I pupil them — they pupil too

as for statistics of pores and hair
like scalp over cobra — to shrinkhead

then what is a country so apprehended
in relation to the medium small town

loves and spores of expellees
displace into a kind of passage — desert

dunno are they well fed and on the stretch
people one meets are never missing legs

their foot region seems bashful to me
yet treading itself is unabashed

undeservedly static — mountain and valley appear
nothing but longtimes there — simply their golgotha

truly exotic in them — my similarity
from time to time expulsed from their illusion

specifically there'd be then a tuftytuft
the sort to be found three houses farther on

at certain spots ventilation becomes a point
but now that's what dustdevil screws are for

whoever's childhood they realized/realize
this country is for me the catcher in the rye's

C. M.

IT'S ON DRY COHESION that the army surgeon pins his handkerchief complete with 'bread-and-butter smell. A giant pencase with snowy circles chains the cactus to the pier — approximating sundried apples. No rebus that would shrink, but 56 strokes per minute (sardines in oil) equal precisely the fraction of a mile... let us now take to heart along the hill with sawed-off shotguns, and from iodine and evil flee into our washbags briefly — at the expense of sunset red, the surgeon makes himself scarce brownstone: O hair curlers... let us together lean against hydrants, horny infants, seals, pompous messages on tallow, toast and rifle up to the remote cuntrol of crosshair mass for which all seven lines — his handkerchief is steamy.

R. W.

HE WHO IS WITHOUT LEAST ACID among you let him be the first to lift his eye: id heat shield, id de feat, id wind supply — convex, concave, ventoux... As in great science fiction: day moon flips over the horizon into the catch-all basin — Europe, dizzy, all the way to Mars. And onto heights depths heather volatile automatism falls, from a great idstance the ball of shadow quantity, my quilted hem stitched: et tu, canal? net? heart's content?

R. W.

CRIMEAN-GOTHIC MARCHING SONG

marimal milliman
assymetrix
minimal marimum

perpetuum zingular
assymer
perpetuar zingulum

solim genistub
azimuttm
woblintschek

hospodar
wendelin
forsooth-balk

epolithic
shrank
even-even

(frantu)

gamilton mass
ventrix
macmachineel

zinger
zinger
vinxinx—

rock mutilar

O. P. /R. W.

SHOCKS IN THE MASON JAR

Three of my home-made eight
dampers come out of my wig
drawer whenever i need them here
i'm lost to them over there

the other five, too, I want back
pronto — travel's
fine but the three on the side
pinch during production

back into their treacherous container
with them not vice versa they at least
squeeze me tight and
keep the pests inside the comb

mornings after seventeen it's
normal that I want them back
my eight migraines — and not just
three parting my hair like rails

R. W.

IDEM

Not one of my eleven
home-made bath salts is soluble
in nature therefore they occur
only in their pure state

to the nationalization of memoirs
and to my efforts on behalf of baths
we've therefore always been
under insoluble hairy obligation

for this economy in particular
we've given up on solidarity
and quick solutions
eleven bath-salts is a lot

nay, for personal reasons
bath-salts are shackles
on the people's desire
for love and closely tied

R. W.

WHAT, HOWEVER, IS the discretion of left to your?
What is never needed by ominable ab? Would swum
have? Too pensive for ex? Suction-cupped over?
Bogeymanhole conspiracy? And why where?

R. W.

THE CONSTRUCTION IS simple: the state of affairs lives in a weather glass — hence there are at least two. Because state of affairs (weather glass) and state of affairs (state of affairs) both feed on insight. This is often annoying because state of affairs jagged, weather glass round. Hence the state of affairs cannot live in either weather glass or singular. It be pretty pigheaded and majestically pity itself: "Poor old frogs."

R. W.

THE FUSION BEGAN at the neck. Artlessness is what counts. In the transition from stylish shift to the undertie of sharp crease research, geology reveals the compound form of "the Kafkasus" — "an obvious, easily imitated weakness of nature, you wouldn't want your dollar bills made like this." OK. But Permethis was not Protheteus. Her thermal baths began in the deciduous forest whereas the ogling muck-cow was settled somewhat higher amid bright biscuitry, pines and propylaea. Inside her maxillar cavity Genoveva shrank venerably down to crumbs — Gallus what a chalk cirrus!

R. W.

MANY GLOVE COMPARTMENTS

of them many are cadaver and the nowadays
over tar and high trail and artificial balm

they live off wild honey and jerky bristleback
frugally in comparison with similar leisurelove

but of a blunt fingernail not a sign at all
but please not a trip of narrative art either

why did the head start to subside at vista point?
the more freshly one returns — a nativity hero

their problem children — high keys deep windows
and the stomach content was fussily stuffed full

they had a car jack and good reason for it
and were lefthanded enough — coital hypnotint

to whom to be tough but nuts robust halfways
a chance at eucalyptus-sigismund is given

and came clucking usefully over shelterbelts
clad to the nines in billboards on reunion road

since they raised no scruple or sworn diagnosis
the balm became brittle — ocean at a hammerswing

C. M.

TRAINING FOR SMALLER BUILDINGS

Large enough to hold an index a hall fills a small
auditorium — A to Z no limits to completeness.
Ready to start position of legs. There are correc-

tions and objections. Even one auditorium fills
a small hall. Let alone the index! Yes, the joy of
holding an index borders on losing one's mind.

By definition, the hall that fills an auditorium
can hold a hall — essentially however the audi-
torium that fills a small hall fulfills nothing

but its purpose. What has happened to the index?
Well even reflections like these will fill an index —
why waste words in addition! No, you'd never

guess all that's still lacking in buildings that both
fill and hold! Let's go to a library. Seized by seizing
on being full, there results fullness of feeling.

Also, small claustrophobic lumps catch in your
throat. No gym hall that would not upset nations.
Even the processors that nightly shuffle around

remote buildings are no tall tales. Large enough
to hold an index, a small fox fills the entire glove.
No A to Z limits to being beside yourself.

R. W.

AMMONITE ANONYMOUS

frau von steinheim has tinnitus in
her ear and long been headicapped

her birdcage has been empty for 250 000
years, yet she lives a life of revelry

from concert-pitch A via budding trumpet
B to thunderstroke one centimeter long

von steinheim's a real flashy girl
and her tinnitus an eyeful wretch

under cypresses in high wind he mounts
her nitrogen Jura and circulation

but there's a roar in her cochlea oh
oh she has misconceptions all her own

and with body and hole is no more than
a small cephalopod complete with extinct earwig

R. W.

CANDIDE

With eyes open, he continues, act just for once as if
you'd been somewhere; forget just tentatively where;
then act as if it had occurred somewhere to someone —

forget, occurs to him, he continues, that it's just ten-
tatively you forget, eyes open, what you once
knew before you'd been somewhere; therefore continue

to act as if you'd only sometime now and then
been somewhere — he, it strikes him, never once forgot
to assume he was somewhere, let alone there; as if

he didn't know, listen, he assumes, that it was
obviously him — no eyewitness, no; what an idea;
you'll see where you've omitted what; and even if

you do forget, look out; something somewhere you've seen
and heard and forgotten who you've been — just act as if
you don't, for all that, ever think, let's say, of New York

City — then it will perhaps occur to you where
you've perhaps been; it's true, I do not know if any-
thing more will then occur to you, forget about it; even

if you sometime now and then are somewhere; listen,
it seems to me you've been somewhere; don't act as if
you hadn't noticed; you should — just tentatively — know.

R. W.

71

ONE MOLECULE TINNITUS plus one molecule tinnitus equals one molecule tinnitus. Plus one more molecule tinnitus plus one more molecule tinnitus equals one more molecule tinnitus. But no further molecule tinnitus plus no further molecule tinnitus equals one further molecule tinnitus. Just as one molecule tinnitus plus no molecule tinnitus equals one molecule tinnitus; and no molecule tinnitus plus one molecule tinnitus another one. Not one molecule tinnitus but no molecule tinnitus equals one molecule tinnitus. Neither one molecule tinnitus nor no molecule tinnitus equals one molecule tinnitus. Moreover, never does one molecule tinnitus plus one molecule tinnitus equal one molecule tinnitus; for one as well as none equals one. And even one molecule tinnitus at a distance of several years equals one molecule tinnitus. Never never does one molecule tinnitus ever equal one molecule tinnitus, and never the other way round.

R. W.

WITHIN THE MEANING OF a stipulation getting ready to Gustav leans from Gustav to Gustav on Gustav; dispensing with the image of personality and so peripatetic in horticulture (graineater) on polder-green and polder-black and on the sly he passes a bonus-blend into the pretty little paws of the lay-out — would you keep this for five minutes for your Gustav's Gustav resp. his Gustav's farfetched muzzle; so spider-eating he expresses himself on the counterscarp about the briskly lurching lebensraum of the phlox next to Gustav's Gustav's lower case; of which we brag in ever lousier and vaster forests (peacrocks and martens) all the way to the plural — apart from interpellations from goiter and thimble.

R. W.

— THERE'S A SMELL of chocolate: Arthur as muffler from the right with a chuckleduster in his ear and three comets of varying length (pat, matte, pompous) — the most natural maxims in the world; here they lay, here they lay bare, here they got laid; and here you've got your fingertips in dill (sword-rage, word-sort, wage-cage, broccoli-broth); little popsongs as an aftertaste from the start — Arthur on cord; the dialogue can be skipped; from above, big spot light (ochre, delta, cinnamon) on the whole round breast-market under semantics; add a pile of pudding-blue (bust-cork, soft-bock, golf-wear); local summons/total; under the sideboard there begin to accumulate carvings by Arthur — some müsli, slowly please, as a pet from the left.

R. W.

MOLE IN PROFILE

Engaging in topology a local character may find
entire sectors at his disposal; in one end and
out the other — an omnibus miracle, silly,

but "as in a dram" we may say notwith-
standing. It's startling how the so-
called color plantations function. Even Alex-

ander, for example, was a man of name — one
man one throat. By contrast, the resume "revels"
(tooth out, tuck up — lobotomy), and even seeing-

eye-dogs carry a zipcode. Likewise with likes:
Beckett and Buckow. Ann of Clark Gables not far
behind. Meanwhile the almond tree blooms "as if

freshly soldered." Anyway — is this Berlin? As the
index so the resolution: unnamed features gradual-
ly fade away. As for the rest, the recessed retina

disposes of entire ends, one unlocatable
ginkgo biloba and "three white melons"—
as suggested, a miracle: remote in, remote

out; meanwhile "Musil," "Boston," "Vladivostock."
In terms of place the local can't be topped; it's just
optically that the divan slowly as it were overgrows.

R. W.

MAUSOLEUM! SUCTION CAP! Recruits! The pink mimosas in the piazza pluck and plaice. They have scales like small change, tongue coins — in this place blown godforsaken. But they are really old Eskimos with crew cuts — Wozzecks of the gauntlet! Just wanted to lick icecream. Engrave syllables, copper and dapper, mix whale and lava. Now they hatch carrots, bogeymen, all matter of botany. Anthropothermically they stand at attention on foot and endocrine meltdown — hands on seams. At night when the commandos rest, they pull their rosy fur down over their parts as mimicry and mosey out of this big dick into the solid sauna — Roman dots.

R. W.

FILLING STATION

The Farmer takes the Poet into the grave with him;
the Poet takes the Knight into the grave with him; Castle,
Sensor, and Scene Change are likewise Tro-
phies, which the Castle, the Sensor, and the Scene Chan-
ge take into the Operyhouse — the overture
astounds posterity: in the stovepipe an exchange

of words ignites: until the door swings open the other
way; the Barman takes the Bottle from the Shelf;
generally movie theaters take Old Strangers into
the grave with them — they are, to be sure, Rooms and not Distan-
cings; their sense for Noses hanging from the Flies is more stunt-
ed than their sense for Old Archives; the Farmer

takes the Poet to San Francisco with him, where they
exchange Trophies together — First Aid for
Bishops, Sensors, and Scene Change; here I have nothing
particular in mind; the giving of Names never was
the Question; the road takes the Opera on its shoulders and trundles
home with it; the operetta sleeps the Old Gold Rush off.

C. M.

APPING

e scapes from below, dis integrates from a bove; ap
proaches with heads, be holds the fork; stands end on,
doesn't hoot a give, smokes; the cow pricks up her oars
and moon — flits and takes her time... and prehends
com mountain meadow, re ceives and lieves and comes
calving. after wards and over hangs. bangs intro. duces
de. mands — plores im... winnipeg wins peg — stump
baloney and mine strone together stew a plot. how to
gulate re: roast moon traffic. rumor to attica, tumor to
formica. tinker tailor carrier cause — the ann ouncer
the re tailor the be cause wool in the died. eh! ham-
burger scissorer plumberer butterer hornerer liverer
thunderer runnerer mowerer racketer smokerer. con
fesses from below, be holds from a bove; the cow
pricks up her oars and moon. takes her time. has now,
oc curs, may can, up oil. then goa head and carp a path
a cross a pill. an e mone standing-reportextermitator —
shrill the syllapilgrimchoir!... and hrugs his houlders
(carhorn nightrogen ears appetite) till up rises
unsmeared limp. he cinnamons seniles hounds of pack,
be purrs lies helterskelter and scapes land, biter, bog in
the time of nick qua tor al-el still: preappoc bediscom...

R. W.

IN FRONT OF A BACKGROUND of wild vines growing rank over some construction and in the foreground rising on unsupportive materials out of plankton constantly blocking out a rank and wild background

R. W.

RAVEN SON

O raven son O raven son
the crooked dog the crooked dog
the island wild the island wild
in open fields in open fields

the crooked dog the raven son
the island wild the open fields
the day of the week the day of the week
in open fields the day of the week

the sourdough the sourdough
of raven son of crooked dog
of island wild of open fields
of sourdough of sourdough

the element of elements
the zero of zero of zero sum
the grammophone of grammophones
the raven son of raven son
the bucketkicker's sourdough

the crooked dog in open fields
the saturday of saturday
the grammophone of saturday
of island wild of cruddy dog

the cow the Poo the schmoo the crew
the schmoozing zone of seamy types
of tanks of banks of sourdough
the A of ma of zo of ne

O raven son crude gasoline
go pre app poc go be dis com
O head in hand O open dog
horizon O of cruddy field

R. W.

A PLOT

Tinnitus and Tacitus go with world history
— hand in hand. The pair of lovers they make
is returned to them at the coat check. Then they

are called Herodot and Antidot because of their
high blood pressure. Tinnitus deduces, Tacitus
alludes pointedly. Herodot blows his fuses,

Antidot does not tell all. The pair of lovers they
made and had returned to them now sit
in front of the TV and want some salt. In return,

world history rattles off its lovers from
antiquity, middles ages and modern times.
Others sit on a bench, in reserve, holding

hands. Lots of things happen. The text is
chockfull of lovers. Tinnitus brews infusions,
Tacitus draws conclusions, while Herodot

rakes muck with Antidot. On TV, geography.
All short statements join hands and,
together, clink glasses and effusions.

Blood pressure's contusions in his ear, Tinnitus
roars by Tacitus' mouth. Herodot's tacit turn's a
picture book. Antidot blows kisses to his dregs.

R. W.

————— INTERLUDE

HISTORY, POETRY

History happens; historiography is made. Poetry happens and is made. Where do lean sentences lead? Do slow sentences protect us from the past? From the future? By speaking inadequately I hope to behave adequately: warnings and spells. My vita is history in as far as I exist proportionately — against this automatism I am a minority, as is every other individual. By writing, however, I make a singular move into the majority. Now, where history happens, in facts, there is increase in language. No denial can do away with news. Hindsight reveals its purpose. The time I take to say "I" is the time in which effect turns around and into cause. Even historians are human. Even poetry is news. Yes, I am differently cared for by words and by history; if better remains in question. What matters always is to avoid, in exemplary fashion, any trace of being exemplary — I shudder at the consequences of loose talk of the shavings that supposedly have to fall in the name of history. I shudder at the damage the basic and purposeful logic of my own words is capable of doing, no matter how charmingly it gets in the way of history. By writing against the automatic fear of the automatic I publicly play with the history of automatism. My interest in saying "I" seems to be universal; from this I calculate my chance of doing damage. What poetry is I do not know. With the understanding that I no longer know any gauge I gauge the meaning of sentences which perhaps contains me. Then there are leaps. Then there are no more leaps. In retrospect, poetry degenerates into history.

(*Ingwer und Jedoch*, Herodot, 1985)

R. W.

IV. POEMS 1980-97

MEANING-MANIA IN SAND-SIEVE, WITH ANTIDENTAL-IMAGISM, SKETCH

Wigwam basis likes league of Nice. Parciwhale likes Bali-Lisa —
with cinnamon. Saracen bast salmon likes Vivaldi's I-Ching —
piffle paffle doesn't like sisal. Can Garibaldi zigzag? Never ever
is anis lapidary. Liszt measures anger with carbide. Aspirin
wears shish kebab for hair. Mata Hari loves safari. Radio's Ararat
can be encouraged — where does Rita find her graphite? Vita is
risky... There are four kiwis in the magma — super, super! Ida
agitates in aspic. Tigris perspires with Adi in participle: hic Atlas
— hic salta. Itis Mips eats drips... Is statistics fiddlesticks? Sinti
(astral) squeaks in anagrams, Kafka sneezes, Fickfuck runs,
Mastix mixes syntax in a taxi, nothing happens — Mistral is
nasty. Waikiki intends balalaika. What lies flies — Ali eats grits.
Fiji flashes in transit. Hafiz declares Tristram fit. The fish in the
dish has slipped. Mimicry wheezes in the labyrinth — cryptic
shit: eight times did Bambi bite granite. Papa traffics in lapis
from lazuli to Gibraltar — circa. Scilla is fast. How is Lima? In
cross section pyramidal. What can Niagara not be? Mississippi. Is
Pamir intact? Never. Upshot: by the time the Kalahari twigs
Byzantium it's Kasimir's pirate's turn. Saliva's cock likes to cite
cyclamate. When Billy steps in paprika Manna holds a zinc bath
to his chin. Flavia-Mania strips while Pia riffs in cliffs: ha!
Antsyclapaedia transsylvanica: never was Vienna in four
nirwanas. Tbilisi has the Saar wired — in the beginning was
plaster then faster then disaster (spiral start)... Zumba-Limba as
click-machinist. This here is Bistritz as prism. That there is
primed to flit all the way to Assisi. Franz in canoe is stable too.
Lisa's Titian chirps almost physically. Dill in drill or tapir-paper.
In a rape-lamb Ars Palma is tangible as ram-psalm — Milan in
grass evokes glass-philately: four times before noon. Then Fiat
steps on the gas, lettuce gets less, Dana wants Bambi, Milba plays
ringtoss, ripoff kills simile — Pinxit was here.

R. W.

TWO SONNETBURGERS

Song of the Mermaid in Distress

no she never ate asparagus
I suppose she ate spinach
of flagella-leguminose
but no asparagus never

yes she was always genuine
and never ever hungry
let alone hormone-beset
and parsimonious she was

but no she never ever rode
anything but a toothbrush
and was never never full

she had to wash the celery
out of the spinach and her
chair was so uncomfortable

The Yob has Two Gels

oval hill and oval dale
hillal vulval naval hill
da ovaltail da ovaltail
oval oval hill and dale

oval oval dale and hill
valhal hillal va and va
naval oval do and hale
oval office hah offhill

waval-ho to waval-hill
holehill dadale and dado
hillhill volli vola-dale

vernal taletale sale ohale
waval-woe to lilac vale
oval oval hole and hole

R. W.

88

ABRACADABRA

abracadabra as was
tartar, as was kandahar-
cardan (tack that man and gal
flat as washrags!), as was cash
cadav-bag, as was macad-
am-madam, and Kamchatka
(that anagram was banal)

perfect steel fetters defend
the element's element,
when even pesterers (beep-
beep, beep-beep!) engender these
deepened well-essences; then
nettlebeds redeem the hell
where chester cheeses breed (bet?)

if in wilds iltis is striv-
ing with sissi — is it im-
pinging? Inspiring tri-mi-
ni-kids. Sissi's rimini-
kilt-itch stirs him. In this biz,
big risk: in hindsight it's tick-
lish, Sissi's biting "finish!

no-color o-moo-cocoon
spools pro lotto for wood-rod:
on spot of god pollock's cold,
chloroform stops motor-knock,
solo moons don't brood, or prows
slow-cook loco (on dock) — or
songs bow down to protocol

ur-cur trusts sulfur baths: plush
cult buff. up church hulk, duck hung —
bull guru struck dun — glum slump
turns, unstuck sulk burns: tumult
trust sunk! ruth hums, plumb tug un-
stuck, truthful-dumb bunk-buzz. sum
up? just cuscus rush; just rush!

H. M.

WITH DULLED MOLD THE ALL
too heavy porcelain cyclamen
will bedouin with genuine from
pelargonia cover from within
like gongtormented infusoria
that urinate on ruins into snails
or kunigundulate from lyotards
a thumbline whose malvaceous
larvae like cycladic oysters
feed on avalanches of glycinia

R. W.

CALLAS — THISBE — NERO

dramatic echelon
amassing stereo
balsam in the metro
backpacks l'idée of
March atilt even so
grace has its effect on
arms said seen to-
ward pairs tended toc-
cata in evensong
salami the epos
a tragic event yo-
ga active effort
grammar bilevel Rohr-
schach addict envelops
lamas in nests ergo
an Achilles tendon
awaits the Epsom
salts' acid test telos
alarming except O-
mar Sharif then enrolls
as almsbitter endstop

R. W.

HOW SHALL I NOW in turn call or bring this question into answer, or do only things syntactic turn and return my, please, thanks without guarantee of fear, without regard for lack of thinking, with process of what if what of process, with thinking of lack, for regard without fear of guarantee, without thanks please my return and turn syntactic things, only do or answer, into question this, bring or call, turn in now, I shall, how?

R. W.

IF THE SOUP IS WHITE

if the soup is white
the spoon must be bent

which is not proper
when a dumpling's slurped

how do you like it
when belinda groans

come on upstairs
till the skullbone comes

for the pot will break
if it is taken

so the bulb will keep
if it is taken

for the pot will break
till the skullbone comes

come on upstairs
when belinda groans

how do you like it
when a dumpling's slurped

which is not proper
the spoon must be bent

if the soup is white

R. W.

IRREVERSIBLE? IS TIME — were it as itself — reading underneath the influence of palindromitis? Or what is it, earlier or later, with or without authority, that probably determines orientation — and beats the record? Perhaps without memory and imagination; nevertheless this is something no-one says. Therefore syntax solely noway works it. No money as consolation or innocence imprisoned — mere relationship. Against vagueness, reading too quickly thereby creates otherwise former procedure as rewind. And definitely bending sentences snip syllables wherever it is heading. Aha! *heading*, is it? Wherever syllables snip sentences (bending definitely!) and rewind as procedure (former "otherwise") creates "thereby" — quickly, too. Reading vagueness "against" relationship, mere imprisoned innocence, or consolation as money? No! it works. Noway solely syntax. Therefore (says no-one), something is this neverheless: imagination and memory, without "perhaps," record the beats, and orientation determines (probably) that authority, without or with (later or earlier) "it is." What "or" (palindromitis) of influence, the underneath? Reading itself, as it were, time is irreversible.

H. M.

FEE ZONE

dustfee guiltfee heatfee
smoke break wrinkle postage fee
fee block fee alliance scotfee
duty school spot germ and carefee
fee church fee city coinage company fee trader
feedman and woman energy
fee fall and for all floating fugue

the land of the fee

feedom of thought fratern- and equal
fee love time style fee will
feedom of movement of religion
fee association mason lance
fee air balloon bid board booter
feewheeling fee and easy

on fee day the rabbi slept late

the feedom of press speech and assembly
demands a fee translation in fee verse
fee people country goods and enterprise
leadfee gasoline fee passage port and services
feeborn fee chapel fee of charge
we must be fee or die

fee drinks for fee thinkers

God created the mind fee and fee it shall remain
fee soil, feestanding, -spoken men, fee market
nicotin- and fatfee riskfee fee
of prejudice or error rent fee fee of additives
feeway fee zone and waters
political and intellectual feedom and
feedom of expression is no half-and-half affair
but lovers of feedom must pay the fee of doubt

R. W.

BLE

(for franz mon 1986)

when the parade horse horses through the parade
and dise like digms abound in ox

when llels lipomena go to the pet in guay
with noia meters pluie and sol

O clete — then ffin phrases phernalia
(bles of plegiac keets troop to the llax)

because the gon must chute and feed the sites
and bolicly the graph rides lysis to the mount

R. W.

HAMLET/INLET/AMNESIA

animation. a velvet watch carnation milks a mnemotekel. iddí samnoí — amid merry elimination-emphasis nomadic mentor agamemnon mendels anemic iambs. coming soon what whom. with amrum/ninive in the monastories mister no jobs his do. now end morains mutter about an omnimalign dream bus dog with truss beam. maniacs with nagging snagedemas mimic the stomach of the numismatic meniscus — the monads are coming. nemesis hems mantles.

for many a man's breath is taken away by the tamtam. philomena minus norm llfully skims amundsen off menelaus. emnid recommends empanadas which clear out the attempt at ethical phonemes. on meeting salmons they button their mutton. with heartrending heartthrobs they mend hollows from unnamed space to unmanned ramses — only miniatures rhyme. ludmilla camomile in tbilissi. monohormonal nominates hymen from yemen an abdominal monsoon after totemic notes: at least michimadigan, anamnesis. hymns in hyannis disarm the little snotnose's presumed instrumentirritation and muzzle his indited benightedness with unguentampons. themes schemes. a mere emmenthal is countered by elastic specimens of mercy, namely chimneyledge and meningitis in enigma. enclosed montanara, lonjam and crumbs.

chemnitz and memphis laminate pneumatically — a sailor's tick. gymnasiums cause misgivings to no one. nimbus diminishes enigma. amnesty clears mines. anomaly is elementary.

for mundane corn pones — a gnome! but lemmings for the hippodrome! for numerical molassis our glassy lindenmasses! once more, phimotic synapses are monitored by osmanli columns. then minona unamuno culminates toward malta. while mothballing somnambulant balsamic snakes nymphomaniacs luminously manipule comembranes. lameness calms mewling at noon — at the new moon a demon spins foamneed, nimrod spans, endymion mimes murnau, a fulminant cantatamorph — smyrna!

still negligence tone-mass takes its feminine, cinnamon runs in the family, manes comb heavy metal chimeras minus a minimum of minne. they streamline machiavelli into mackintosh. elementoupee.

R. W.

THE THINKING OF CHANCE

aside from quenching thirst
the hearing of the genitive
is the garters of knowledge

the bestowal of an ear
the doctor's order

the visit of the cold lady
the sighting of the sighted

"what do you hear with if i have no mouth?"

the law of the home-knit in genuine causalad
the caws of effect in dangling limbs

"do lath floors have a chance?"

—says prestabil to indeterm
(the baxer anecdote seems quite a hit)
while the chique audience applauds

but flatus' fate
boxes the ears of the date

alarmin disarmin and determin shrink
lizard runs to ruin of luck

the encounter is faustian
blather and weather
clock- and cloudwise

aside from drinking blood
the accident of thought
is the invention of a poltergeist

"what are you talking with in case i hear you?"

R. W.

O-TONE "AUTOMNE" — LINGUISTIC AUTUMN

O-tone "automne" — linguistic autumn
Stick harvest / Osenj / Toamna / stick
Stick lipstick nota bene — hay
All that absents itself from dumbbell sermons:

Zero-phoneme

The pumpkin grows
In eros-shirts scythe
Tristia
Trestia
Delta web

There is ("Kusneitschik/Yabigshot") synopsis
Come from Colchis:
Waterlilylake / waterlilybay
East-West-phantom
Ovid's Metamorphoses
At the Bösendorfer Bog

Semaphors morse along:
    "conditions they are bald / by the skin of our tee
    we're banging on / to save our peck
    the year it yeareth /on till gone"

O zero Osero — the sea
Rien ne va plus — O zero stick
O lambda duck groats hair nest falfa
half shelf
hay help
O-tone
Automne
I feel so rosident phantom
Semiramis / Sorbonne / Za-Um-Brella

                                        R. W.

DOMINOTAURUS

dominotaurusbekistandrogynecologistigmamasto
donauberginereidentaluminumbergenitalentrante
penultimathulethargypsychodramabelcantopicto
graphicalibertinagelatincanuterintesticularboreal
penstockmarkettlesterlinguanomenclavemariascle
piusageoldtimermaidenheadstarterrinebuchadnez
zarathustrapezebrandishwasherballustradebility
cooneandertalmudslidemiteflondonquixotempo
ratatouillerriennevapluperfectodermatitisepiano
stradamuscletterpressuresistancestralepharpoti
pharaocarinavigatoreador

R. W.

TODAY'S ARITHMETIC

at ten i was ten
at twenty around thirty
at thirty barely twenty

forty was forty but not years
fifty was sixty minus ten
sixty was fifty plus ten

when my mother was born my father was nine
when my mother was forty i was half that

when i died i was over sixty
when i was over sixty my father was over thirty

and my mother over three

when i learned rithmetic i was under ten
when i was under ten i was born

R. W.

OULIPIAN DERIVES FROM OULIPO: SO

Oulipo,
cool flea! Old
moose-itch coat,
should we go
shoe-in-nose
too? We? No!
Urinose
spoor gleans most
ruby. So
you pick whole
views which (cold
fury, tor-
turing) pole —
buteo
moves (Tyrol
moos) with own
tune which no
hood will hole...
You live so
"oulipo,"
poo! We pro-
duce things so
you read "own
fuse" — still, mod-
moon Kienholz-
brood steers home...
Look: here's loam
to bring... oh,
pooped, its clone
droops. It scolds:
move, philo-
doopsio!
Dubbio —
cook me, stove
Oulipo!

H. M.

104

—————— INTERLUDE

SKETCH

Can literature speak for itself? This sentence can evidently be written. And not only this. Posed as a question it may, because in it "literature" "conceives" of "itself" as a subject capable of action and statement, "of course" (i.e. because "language" as a matter of course supplies instruments that think for you, including "the contrary") be considered a mere claim: literature is capable of speaking for itself.

Literature thinking or speaking for itself is therefore absolutely thinkable. It can claim so, and we likewise, because people accept it. The personal union within the aforementioned instruments make this possible for it and us. Literature acts like a person, and so, in analogy, do we. "We" are therefore dealing with anthropomorphic processes.

Nothing human is alien to literature. It can speak for itself, but does not have to. It can also speak for others, e.g. for secondary literature or the author. It can also speak for the publisher. It speaks for literature that it not only can speak but can also be silent and read.

Does something that can speak for itself, be silent and read, need to be spoken for? Or, put differently: to what extent would speaking for it, assuming that literature needs it, be a different language from the one literature does not need because it has it, otherwise it would not exist? In my opinion, speaking for it can count on a large public, and more. As for speaking for it, it does not care if literature needs it or not — rather it needs literature in order to be what it is, namely speaking for it.

While literature pretends to be dumber than it is in order to stress its humanity which need not to be spoken for, speaking for it is actually very intelligent: it forgives the measliness of its forewords.

So there is probably more at stake. Literature says it without using it. Speaking for it uses "it" by saying "it." Literature with built-in speaking for it...

(*Jalousien aufgemacht*, Carl Hanser, 1987)

R. W.

V. A SMALL ARTISTIC MACHINE

Sestinas

Eine kleine Kunstmaschine:
34 Sestinen
(Carl Hanser) 1994 ——

AN ALTOGETHER REMARKABLE ITEM

"that there might exist a language in which falsehood could
never be spoken or, at least, any dent in the truth would
make a dent in grammar as well"
—Georg Christoph Lichtenberg

A small artistic machine fashioned with an undescribable cylinder
has three what might be referred to as "positionings,"
to explain which it brings three distinct systems into action,
in an emergency no more sizable than a cause;
a more than half transparently fashioned bellows,
as well as space for two or three other windmill vanes.

Occasionally, on the left windmill vane,
a body and a soul are erected by means of which the cylinder
could also be extracted; but in that case the bellows
and the preordained harmony must be directed to positionings
at a certain distance from the so-called double cause
and, with somewhat faulty steadfastness, be imparted to the action

of their miniature limbs in this manner — no action
of over 4 to 5 inches would then tear the windmill vanes
to shreds; similarly might the influence and cause
of an ant blowing with steadfastness explain the precious cylinder
by way of two or three physical positionings
of the crank in the precious ancillary bellows.

At a certain distance, no larger than the bellows,
it would occasionally be necessary to explain that action,
made of finest horn; just as in a minor emergency the positionings
of the so-called "endless screw" in the windmill vanes
(i.e. attached through the influence of the system to the cylinder)
could be extracted from the lengthy cause

of the imparted handiwork (such is the name of the cause
at a certain distance) - provided that from the bellows
a soul and a body also be extracted and that, on its cylinder,
by means of the occasionally half-transparent action
made of somewhat faulty ivory, a windmill vane
be erected with a view to so-called "double positionings."

Consequently at two to three preordained positionings
a goldbeater's skin would be torn to shreds; directed by no cause,
no more sizable than a sizable windmill vane,
three distinct ants would bring the bellows
into the horn and, with flawed steadfastness, the distance into action
to an inch made out of the familiar harmony of the long-lasting cylinder.

Occasionally, on the left windmill vane,
a screw and a horn are erected and the so-called cylinder
blown; in this case, however, the crank has no bellows.

H. M.

this sees said six so as
as this sees said six so
said six so as this sees
so as this sees said six
six so as this sees said
sees said six so as this

here six there in that sees
sees here six there in that
there in that sees here six
that sees here six there in
in that sees here six there
six there in that sees here

six so in that sees here
here six so in that sees
in that sees here six so
sees here six so in that
that sees here six so in
so in that sees here six

so as that sees here six
six so as that sees here
that sees here six so as
here six so as that sees
sees here six so as that
as that sees here six so

as this sees here six so
so as this sees here six
sees here six so as this
six so as this sees here
here six so as this sees
this sees here six so as

says said six so as this
this says said six so as
six so as this says said
as this says said six so
so as this says said six
said six so as this says

six there in that here sees
sees here six so as that
six so as this said says

H. M.

SESTINA WITH INTERVIEW

oh of course I was often a second time
in rome — but at certain times I was also
actually there for the third or fifth time. when were
you there the last time? that I can in fact
specify: it was when for the first time I went away.
but since then were you ever again in rome?

no the first time I was to be sure still in rome
but not constantly more often like the second time —
that did not occur until after once there I went away.
but your last time in rome were you also
constantly thinking of actually going away? in fact
I always constantly think of it often: if ever you were

such a one there who often went away, you were
at certain times also quite definitely not in rome.
but do you also constantly realize when in fact
you at certain times and actually at which certain time
had to go away and as a consequence of this also
wanted to at a time there when nothing else went away?

well you see when for the first time there I went away
I hadn't realized that yet. But you were
at certain times then often a third time also
there again without ever going away at a time in rome
when nothing else went away? no it was the second time
that happened — at certain times I still realize that in

since you see actually I so constantly was often in fact
in rome that at certain times I in no way went away
because not even once had I the first time
gone away. no wait a minute so you were
actually once after that truly in rome?
certainly — actually you see I was still there also

and constantly was without any interruption also
there a second and third time just in fact
like the last time I was once again in rome
at a time when nothing else went away.
but tell me that last time in rome were
you in that case actually more often a second time?

oh of course at certain times I was then only one time
in rome before I more and more rarely went away —
because also the last time there it was dark in rome.

H. M.

SESTINA WITH SHIP HOIST

now let us all keenly see for the duration of a hoist
at a torture soupé the two biographical courts
put together; and dancing in, the trough
94 long, 60 high, 27 wide, on a bed
with twelvefold girdles, from one to another dash
low meter mountain music in a powder mantle

the storm locked in a coach in a powder mantle
loses by this bandaging of his eyes with the hoist's
downfallen locks a vast deal; how the dash
lays on — long counterweights, linked by courts
with 4300 tons of water minutes, guess the bed
of black cold worldlings — epicurism in the trough

stands not the giant there like micromegas in the trough
of the body politic? seized was he by the powder mantle
steel-reinforced towering over a bed
just as high, just as stiff and stark? the hoist's
slab duration is five natures flat over the courts
leaf by leaf, its long dash

to bind on the old taffeta ribbon — dash —
and prink for all maybeings the ship trough
by rack and pinion, milliomillio's courts —
the very name Rack opened a powder mantle
to him like a melon under its bell of the hoist
the child grew full of love on a bed

22 mm thick as a leader in the dance from one bed
to another, the power source was for him a dash;
where the wheat ear and the cluster and the olive hoist
often as if together raise on a pulley the trough
and lower it, one sees there the powder mantle
crumble 36 meters deep, over swelling courts

the dangerous bird-pole of these artificial courts
dancing in — and don't you see there the bed
of the sluice height robed in a powder mantle?
that he thus guessed the tulip tree's sparkling dash
with fifty-fifty baptismal and funeral bells per trough
and Borromean books before the lace mask of a hoist

how beautiful, and then the bandage of a hoist
seized him 86 m long overwhelming wide and with the trough
through 256 steel cables and a rack per dash.

C. M.

In its entirety out of the angled incidence (in the "nature of things,"
"that something might be said") — a tangled thing, *un lukru krez*:
something of a coincidence, to think there of Lucretius — thus come
upon, and consulted; the date, the place.
On June 16, 1991, we go — Emily Böhme, Harry Mathews,
Marianne Frisch, the Wichners, and myself — to the ship hoist at
Niederfinow, near Eberswalde, about 70 km northeast of Berlin.
A splendid technical construction, towering unadorned in the land-
scape, and extant from the Bauhaus era. And still in operation.

I read the technical details from the back of the admission ticket:

Date and cost of construction: 1927-34; 27.5 Mill. RM.
          Hoist Frame: 94 m long, 27 m wide, 60 m high.
          Trough: 85 m high, 12 m wide, 2.50 m deep
    Weight when flooded: 4300 tons
    Hoisting height:: 36 m
Hoist duration at 12 cm per second: 5 mins
    Sluice duration: 20 mins
    Counterweights: 4300 tons, connected to trough by 256 steel cables of 52 mm diameter. The cables run over pulleys of 3.50 m diameter, each weighing ca. 5 tons.
    Power source: 4 electric motors, each of 55 kw, raise and lower the trough by rack and pinion.
    Slab: steel-reinforced concrete 20 m thick. The base plate is 4 m thick.

It all clicked when I looked at the bookshelves — Jean Paul, *Titan*, Vol. I.* There, on pages 94, 27, and 60 (corresponding to the measurements of the construction in meters) I found the rest of the language material. Probably the notion of union is rounded off in the time-looping of 39 waterpipes per man and nose.

---

*Manu Verlag, Augsburg, 1948, 2 vols.
Translator's note: the English version derives from Charles Brooks' translation of 1877 (Henry Holt).

C. M.

FIFTH METABOLIC ISTHMUS SESTINA
(After Oskar Pastior)

Sex thought really all there was
Was sex thought really all there
Really all there was sex thought
There was sex thought really all
All thought was there sex really
Thought really all there was sex

Miss really thought you call sex
Sex really miss thought you call
Thought sex call really miss you
Call sex you really miss thought
You call sex miss thought really
Really thought you call sex miss

Telephone makes sex call this miss
Miss telephone makes sex call this
Sex miss telephone this call makes
This miss makes telephone sex call
Call this miss telephone makes sex
Makes sex call this miss telephone

Fakes what sex call forget miss
Miss fakes what sex call forget
Sex call forget miss fakes what
Forget miss what fakes sex call
Call forget miss what fakes sex
Sex call forget what miss fakes

What this sex question call fakes
Fakes what this sex question call
This call fakes what sex question
Question this call fakes what sex
Call question this sex what fakes
Fakes sex this question call what

Sex quiz question who makes what
What sex quiz question who makes
Question who makes what sex quiz
Makes what sex quiz question who
Who makes sex what quiz question
Quiz question who makes what sex

Question quiz really thought was sex
Sex miss makes what is there
Is quiz question who sex fakes

John Yau

BIOGRAPHICAL NOTE

Oskar Pastior was born in 1927 in Hermannstadt, in Siebenbürgen, the German-speaking part of Romania. After the war he, along with other young Romanian-Germans, spent 5 years in a Soviet Labor Camp as part of Romania's reparation for having sided with Hitler. This experience, he says, provided him with his thematic tonic: "the small — but significant — scope between freedom and determinism." Then, after taking a university degree and working for the Bucharest radio, he managed, in 1969, to come to Berlin where he has gained a considerable reputation as a poet, performer and the only German member of OULIPO.

Among books not represented in this selection are *Francesco Petrarca: 33 Gedichte* (1983), *Anagrammgedichte* (1985), *Villanella & Pantum* (2000), and a volume of poetics: *Das Unding an sich* (1994).

He has also written radio plays and translated Khlebnikov and many Romanian writers into German.

His honors include the Peter-Huchel-Prize (2001), Hugo-Ball-Prize (1990) and Ernst-Meister-Prize (1986), a stay at the Villa Massimo in Rome (1984) and an honorary doctorate from the Lucian-Blaga-University in Hermannstadt (2001).

Atlas Press in London has published a larger selection from *Gedichtgedichte* in a translation by Malcolm Green: *Poempoems*, 1990.

Harry Mathews, the only American member of OULIPO, has published translations of poetry by Julien Blaine, André du Bouchet, Jacques Dupin, Pier Paolo Pasolini, Marcelin Pleynet, Georges Perec, Raymond Queneau, Denis Roche, Schuldt, Ungaretti, and Jean-Jacques Viton. His poems have been collected in *Armenian Papers* (Princeton University Press). His latest novel is *The Journalist* (David R. Godine, 1994).

Christopher Middleton's selected verse translations, *Faint Harps and Silver Voices* (Carcanet) appeared in 2000. He is known also for his translations of Nietzsche (1969), Robert Walser (1957, 1969, 1983) and Gert Hofmann (1980s). His latest book of poems, *The Word Pavilion and Selected Poems* (2001) is published in the US by Sheep Meadow Press.

Rosmarie Waldrop has translated Elke Erb, Friederike Mayröcker, Ernst Jandl and, from the French, Edmond Jabès, Emmanuel Hocquard, Jacques Roubaud, etc. Her most recent book of poems is *Reluctant Gravities* (New Directions). Northwestern UP has reprinted her two novels (*The Hanky of Pippin's Daughter* and *A Form/ of Taking/ It All*) in one paperback (2001).